32
Better Barbecues

by Helen Feingold

BARRON'S
Woodbury, New York • Toronto • London • Sydney

All inquiries should be addressed to:

Barron's Educational Series, Inc.
113 Crossways Park Drive
Woodbury, New York 11797

International Standard Book No. 0-8120-5517-9
Library of Congress Catalog Card No. 83-2504

Library of Congress Cataloging in Publication Data
Feingold, Helen.
    32 better barbecues.

(Barron's cooking the easy way series)
    Includes index.
    1. Barbecue cookery. I. Title. II. Title: Thirty-
two better barbecues. III. Series.
TX840.B3F4 1983   641.5′784   83-2504
ISBN 0-8120-5517-9

PRINTED IN THE
UNITED STATES OF AMERICA
3 4 5 6   RAE   9 8 7 6 5 4 3 2 1

Credits

Photography
Color photographs: Bill Helms
Food preparation: Helen Feingold
Stylist: Linda Cheverton
Sources for props: *Steven Stewart* for Gordon
    Foster Antiques, 1322 Third Avenue, New
    York, N.Y. 10021: bowl and plate, p. 20; plate,
    p. 44; bowl, p. 57; plate, p. 22; plate and bowl,
    p. 14; bowl, p. 6. *Lynn Evans* for Gordon Foster
    Antiques, 1322 Third Avenue, New York, N.Y.
    10021: platter, p. 48; platter, p. 57; platter, p.
    58. *Gordon Foster Antiques,* 1322 Third Avenue,
    New York, N.Y. 10021: platter, p. 28. *Pottery
    Barn,* 231 Tenth Avenue, New York, N.Y.
    10011: Stockholm platter and plate, p. 10;
    Stockholm platter and plate, p. 56; Galaxy plate,
    p. 34; Stockholm platter, p. 18; Bauhaus plates,
    p. 8; Hellerware, p. 34; Wheatstone platter, p.
    50; Garland plate, p. 36; Arzberg platter and
    plate, p. 26; pitcher and glasses, p. 8. *Manhattan
    Ad Hoc,* 842 Lexington Avenue, New York,
    N.Y. 10021: Sigma platter, p. 16; Sigma platter,
    p. 58; glass, p. 12; Sigma platter, p. 40; Buffalo
    china plate, p. 40; board, p. 6; serving knife and
    fork, p. 50. Flowers by *Howe Floral,* 171 West
    23 Street, New York, N.Y. 10011.

Food consultant Helen Feingold is a well-known
    food consultant with over thirty years'
    experience in the many facets of recipe
    development and food preparation.

Cover and book design Milton Glaser, Inc.

Series editor Carole Berglie

INTRODUCTION

Try the Mexican country back ribs, those meaty sections coated with a tomato-pepper sauce. Or have the crisp-skinned chicken with its moist, juicy flesh just begging to be revealed. Or is it time to sample the crusty grilled lamb, heady with the scent of garlic and herbs? Barbecue—that fundamental cooking of meats, fish, and fowl over an open fire—was a necessity to primitive peoples but it can be an inspiration for modern-day cooks. You can barbecue the always-popular hotdogs and hamburgers, of course, but next time why not substitute game hens, or swordfish steaks, or even a roast fresh ham?

In this collection are 32 ideas for unusual barbecues: a sirloin steak encrusted with salt to seal in the juices and keep the meat tender; innocent-looking hamburgers with surprise stuffings; curried and fruited kabobs of lamb; Texas-style barbecue served up on a toasted bun; and Tabasco-spiced shrimps, threaded on a skewer and grilled until smokey.

Almost every country has some form of grilling their food, but only in America has it developed into a national pastime. This truly American style of cooking probably has its strongest roots reaching back to early Spanish colonists, who settled in the South and Southwest. It explains why so many barbecue sauces have a spicy base.

The Indians were already grilling and smoking meats when the explorers arrived on these shores, but the Spaniards added the sauces that have led to what we generally view as that drippy, lip-smacking barbecue today. Gradually there developed a preference in the South for barbecuing pork, as black cooks also added some hot spices from Africa, while farther West in Southern California and Texas people were barbecuing mostly beef. Thus evolved a crucial matter that splits the country: pork or beef?

The choice is yours. Maybe your family prefers chicken to beef or pork. Barbecuing is not strictly for meat, as many of the recipes in this book will testify. You might also grill vegetables, as accompaniments to be baked in foil or skewered alternately with the meat, fish, or chicken. Meats grill superbly, although the slower cooking needed for larger cuts will give them more time to take on a rich, smokey flavor. Fish is delicate, but also easily picks up a smokey flavor. And poultry lends itself to almost limitless possibilities for flavorings and grilling methods. The sauces you baste with or the marinades you choose to tenderize and flavor your foods can vary also, depending upon whether you like a subtle oriental flavor, a fruity sweet accent, a Southern mustardy coating, or a Tex-Mex firey crispness.

The essence of barbecue is the smokey flavor that comes from cooking over hot coals (not flames!), but you can achieve that with a simple, small hibachi as easily as with a large and expensive gas-fired grill. Costly equipment is not necessary, but for more involved barbecuing you may want a unit with a rotisserie or a dome lid for roasting. The equipment you choose will come with instructions from the manufacturer; follow them.

Barbecuing is most often a backyard affair, but if you lack the patio or deck or lawn, you need not deprive yourself of these finger-lickin' delights. The recipes in this book can easily be adapted to indoor broiler or oven cooking. Just mix the sauce as directed and baste or marinate as for the grill. If you want a mild smokey flavor, add a small amount of Liquid Smoke (available in most supermarkets) to the mixture. This is a concentrate, made by condensing the smoke from hickory wood. It is natural, safe, and a plus for the indoor barbecuer.

C.B.

BETTER BARBECUES

What magic does the great barbecue cook employ to achieve those crusty, succulent results? Proper techniques, applied in a step-by-step manner. Regardless of whether you grill over charcoal or use an electric or gas grill with ceramic or volcanic rock coals, your barbecue does not have to be a smoke signal to the neighborhood. (But the delicious aromas wafting across to their yards will probably start them lighting their grills!)

With gas or electric grills the heat is temperature-controlled to produce foolproof results just by

following the manufacturers' directions. When using charcoal, however, take care to build the fire correctly. Be ready at least an hour before your guests will arrive or before you plan to start cooking, and line the grill pan with a layer of heavy-duty foil to make clean-up easier afterwards ①. Be certain you have enough charcoal, and that you have assembled all the utensils and ingredients you will need.

BUILDING THE FIRE

Charcoal is sold loose in briquet form or molded into paper units resembling an egg carton. You will need about 30 coals for an average barbecue, more if you plan to roast a large piece of meat or turkey.

You will also need a starter. You could use an electric starter, a coil-type instrument that plugs into an ordinary outlet. This coil heats up the coals until they ignite, but then you must remove the coil. Liquid starters and jelly starters also work well, igniting the coals so that they get hot enough to burn steadily.

Place your grill in an area away from the wind, because sudden gusts can lower the temperature of the coals when you cook. Heap the loose briquets in a mound in the center of the grill pan. If using a liquid starter, soak about 6 of the briquets until they stop bubbling, and then place them on the bottom of the mound. If you are using a jelly starter, place 4 to 5 teaspoons into the crevices in the mound of charcoal. Set the coals aflame.

If you are using an electric starter, place coals in a mound on top of it ②, and remove it as soon as the coals begin to burn. When using the paper-covered charcoal, just put a single layer on the bottom of the grill pan, set aflame, and let burn until the paper disappears.

When the coals are hot, spread them in an even layer over the bottom of the grill pan ③. Getting them hot will take about 20 to 40 minutes, but by then the coals will be covered with a gray ash. Gray coals produce a radiant heat with a temperature of about 400° to 450° F., which cooks foods without outer burning. (If using an electric or gas grill, you'll find these are calibrated for proper temperature control.) A simple way to test the heat level is to hold your hand at the cooking height above the coals. When the coals are hot, you will only be able to hold your hand for 2 seconds; when they are medium, 4 seconds; when low, 5 seconds. When the fire is hot, you are ready to cook.

GRILLING TIPS

For best results, you need a steady, hot fire that will cook your food through to your degree of doneness without burning the outside. Set the food on the grill and follow the instructions in the recipes regarding turning and coating with sauce. Generally if your barbecue sauce contains a large amount of sugar or other sweetener, you should brush it on the food after it is almost cooked to prevent excessive burning. Keep a sprinkler bottle or squirt gun filled with water handy to put out any flare-ups caused by fatty drips. In addition, foods that are likely to drip a lot should be placed on the grill rack with a drip pan underneath made of a double thickness of foil. When starting the fire, set the drip pan in and arrange the coals around the pan.

Place thicker foods on the grill rack raised to its highest setting, so the meat can cook slowly all the way through. For a richer smokey flavor, add a few damp wood chips such as apple, hickory, bourbon barrel wood, or mesquite to the coals. Cover the food with a lid or tent of foil and cook as usual. Especially when cooking something that takes a long time, tap the coals from time to time to remove the ash and raise the temperature. If you need to add more coals, fire them in an old pan and then add them to the outer edge of the grill.

Most barbecuing is done in the warm weather, when cooking indoors would heat up the kitchen to an unbearable extent. So if you are cooking something on the grill, plan your meal so that other items can be done on the grill as well. And use the fire to also heat sauces for your barbecue. Then, when you have finished cooking your main dishes, use the coals as they cool to grill fruits or toast pound cake and marshmallows.

EQUIPMENT

Charcoal grills vary, from a simple portable grill or hibachi to a hooded grill with rotisserie, chuck wagons with attached tables, kettle grills, and smokers. Choose the one that suits your barbecuing habits the best.

Other items are also useful, such as heat-resistant spatulas and tongs, which have long handles for reaching into the coals or over the very hot fire. You'll want to consider having ready sauce brushes, spoons, pancake turners, and carving sets. Grill baskets that open to hold foods that are small and hard to turn, such as fish and franks, are inexpensive but valuable if you make such meals. Heatproof skewers are available which hold chunks of food, and they come with racks to hold the skewers as well. Barbecue mitts are most useful when they are well padded and reach to the elbow. Barbecue aprons of heavy washable or leakproof materials are essential, but they can also be a humorous touch when emblazoned with the name of the chef.

IN CONCLUSION

Be innovative with your barbecues. Expensive foods are not always the most interesting to barbecue and to eat. Poultry, sausages, cold cuts, fruits, vegetables, breads, fish and shellfish, ground beef, pork chops, and game all gain added flavor when cooked on a grill. In all cases, from the simplest grill to the most complicated barbecue cart or smoker, follow the manufacturers' instructions for use and care of the grill. Test kitchens spend plenty of time to keep consumers happy, so make the effort to read these booklets before you start cooking. Only then will there be no more burnt offerings, but rather crusty food with that irresistible charcoal-broiled flavor.

YIELD
6 to 8 servings

PREPARATION
10 minutes

MARINATING
30 minutes

GRILLING
50 minutes

INGREDIENTS

1 boneless sirloin steak, 3 inches thick, about 4 to 5 pounds

⅓ cup each corn oil and prepared mustard

Coarse salt, about 1 cup

2 tablespoons cracked black peppercorns

Trim excess fat from steak. Slash the fatty edge of the steak to keep it from curling ①.

Mix oil and mustard and spread it in a thick layer over the steak, top and bottom ②.

Mix salt with pepper and coat steak with mixture, pressing the layer firmly onto the steak ③. Place steak on wax paper and let stand for 30 minutes at room temperature.

Place steak 6 inches above gray coals and grill for 20 minutes on each side for rare, 25 minutes for medium. Use tongs to turn the steak to keep from piercing the meat.

Break the crust from the steak and cut meat into thin slices across the grain. Serve as is or on rye bread toast. Good with corn relish, baked potatoes with chive butter, and beefsteak tomatoes.

YIELD
6 servings

PREPARATION
10 minutes

MARINATING
Overnight

GRILLING
1 hour

INGREDIENTS
6 pounds pork country back ribs
Salt and pepper
Garlic powder
4 cups tomato juice
Juice of 3 limes
2 teaspoons salt
¼ cup steak sauce
½ teaspoon ground cumin
2 teaspoons red pepper flakes
1 teaspoon ground celery seeds
1 tablespoon chili powder

Separate pork into individual ribs and cut off excess fat ①. Sprinkle meat with salt, pepper, and garlic powder.

Mix remaining ingredients ② in a shallow pan or deep bowl. Add ribs and turn to coat well ③. Refrigerate overnight.

Drain ribs, reserving marinade. Place ribs on grill 8 inches above gray coals. Grill for 1 hour, turning and brushing ribs with reserved marinade every 10 minutes.

If desired, heat remaining marinade and serve spooned over each serving. This is drippy eating, so have plenty of napkins available. Serve with marinated artichoke hearts, black olives, and pimientoes; and tortillas warmed on the grill.

DIABLO CHICKEN WINGS

3

YIELD
4 servings

PREPARATION
5 minutes

MARINATING
1 hour

GRILLING
20 minutes

INGREDIENTS
3 pounds chicken wings, tips removed
  and discarded
1 tablespoon coarse salt
1 teaspoon paprika
½ teaspoon red pepper flakes
½ teaspoon garlic powder
1 teaspoon onion powder
1 teaspoon lemon pepper

Wash chicken wings and pat dry with paper towels ①.

Mix remaining ingredients in a large bowl. Add wings and toss to coat all pieces with salt mixture ②. Let stand at room temperature for 1 hour.

Shake off excess seasonings ③ and place chicken wings on grill 8 inches above gray coals. Grill for 8 minutes on each side. Serve with grilled zucchini slices, and a potato salad with oil and vinegar dressing.

YIELD
10 franks

PREPARATION
15 minutes

GRILLING
20 minutes

INGREDIENTS
1 pound (10) frankfurters
2 large dill pickles, cut into 10
    lengthwise strips
10 strips bacon
10 frankfurter buns
20 slices american cheese
½ cup catsup
2 tablespoons well-drained pickle
    relish

Slash the frankfurters lengthwise and open out ①. Place a strip of pickle on each frankfurter. Close and wrap each in a bacon slice, then fasten ends with toothpicks ②.

Place the franks on the grill 8 inches above gray coals, and grill for 10 minutes or until bacon is crisp. Turn franks every 3 to 4 minutes.

Open out frankfurter buns and place them cut side down on the grill; toast them for 2 to 3 minutes. Turn and top each roll with 2 overlapping cheese slices ③. Toast rolls another 2 to 3 minutes.

Mix catsup and relish in a bowl. Remove the toothpicks from the franks and place franks on buns. Top with some of the catsup mixture. Close buns and serve. Serve with cherry tomatoes and potato chips heated on grill.

5

YIELD

6 servings

PREPARATION

20 minutes

MARINATING

I hour

GRILLING

40 minutes

INGREDIENTS

6 Italian sweet sausage links
6 Italian hot sausage links
6 large minute steaks
6 scallions, trimmed and cut into
    4-inch lengths
I cup Italian salad dressing
1/4 cup olive oil
2 large onions, thinly sliced
I red and I green bell pepper, seeded
    and thinly sliced
I clove garlic, chopped

2 tomatoes, diced
1/2 teaspoon each oregano and basil
Salt and pepper

Prick the sausages and place 8 inches above gray coals (or sauté in skillet on stove). Keep water handy for fat flare-ups on the grill. Grill or sauté for 15 to 20 minutes, turning sausages every 5 minutes until they are evenly browned. Cool.

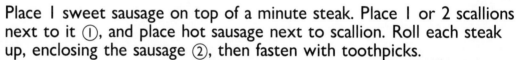

Place I sweet sausage on top of a minute steak. Place I or 2 scallions next to it ①, and place hot sausage next to scallion. Roll each steak up, enclosing the sausage ②, then fasten with toothpicks.

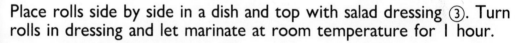

Place rolls side by side in a dish and top with salad dressing ③. Turn rolls in dressing and let marinate at room temperature for I hour.

Drain rolls and place 8 inches above gray coals; grill for 15 to 20 minutes, turning rolls every 5 minutes.

While rolls are cooking, heat oil in a skillet set over coals (or on stove) and sauté onions, peppers, and garlic for 8 to 10 minutes or until wilted. Add the tomatoes, oregano, and basil. Simmer for 10 minutes or until tomatoes are mushy. Season to taste with salt and pepper. Serve steak rolls with vegetables spooned over them. Serve with bread sticks and a watercress and arugula salad.

YIELD
6 servings

PREPARATION
15 minutes

GRILLING
45 minutes

INGREDIENTS
3 broiler-fryers, about 2 pounds each
Salt and pepper

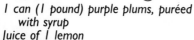

ITALIAN LEMON BASTE ①
1 cup olive oil
¾ cup lemon juice
1 small onion, grated
1 clove garlic, mashed
2 teaspoons paprika
2 teaspoons oregano
2 teaspoons thyme

SPICY TOMATO BEER BASTE ②
1½ cups tomato purée
1 cup beer
¼ cup cider vinegar
3 tablespoons Worcestershire sauce
1½ teaspoons salt
1 teaspoon paprika
½ teaspoon pepper

PURPLE PLUM BASTE ③
1 can (1 pound) purple plums, puréed
   with syrup
Juice of 1 lemon
1 small onion, grated
3 tablespoons sugar
3 tablespoons corn oil
1 teaspoon salt

You will probably want to make just 1 baste for the 3 chickens. Choose your baste, then combine the ingredients in a bowl and mix until well blended (see photos).

Season chicken with salt and pepper. Place chicken 8 inches above gray coals and broil for 15 minutes, turning chicken every 5 minutes.

Brush chicken with baste, turning and brushing every 5 minutes. Grill chicken for another 20 to 25 minutes. Brush chicken with baste, turning and brushing every 5 minutes.

If any baste remains, heat it on the grill and serve it over the chicken. Serve with corn on the cob and foil-baked zucchini and tomatoes.

17

YIELD
6 servings

PREPARATION
25 minutes

GRILLING
10 minutes

INGREDIENTS

1 red and 1 green bell pepper, cut in half and seeded
3 large onions
1 clove garlic
¼ cup butter or margarine
1 tablespoon prepared mustard
1 ring Polish sausage, about 1½ pounds
1 green or red cabbage, or ½ half head of each
½ cup mayonnaise

2 teaspoons lemon juice
Salt and pepper
6 hero rolls, split

Thinly slice the red and green peppers; slice the onions thinly; and slice or chop the garlic into thick pieces ①.

Place a skillet 6 inches above gray coals and melt the butter. Add and sauté the onions, garlic, and peppers until tender, about 10 to 15 minutes. Stir in the mustard and set aside.

Cut the sausage into 6 pieces, then cut each piece in half ②. Place the sausage pieces on the grill and grill for 5 minutes on each side or until golden brown.

Meanwhile, shred the red and/or green cabbage for the slaw ③. Mix together the mayonnaise and lemon juice, then toss with the cabbage.

Toast the hero loaves on the grill.

Place the sausage pieces on the bottoms of the rolls. Top with pepper mixture and roll-tops. Serve at once with cole slaw and dill pickles.

YIELD
6 servings

PREPARATION
5 minutes

MARINATING
1 hour

GRILLING
20 minutes

INGREDIENTS
6 swordfish steaks, 1 inch thick, about 3 pounds

MARINADE
½ cup olive oil
1 cup dry white wine
Juice of 1 lemon
1 small onion, minced
2 teaspoons each salt and oregano
1 clove garlic, pressed or minced

Place steaks into a shallow glass dish.

Mix marinade ingredients ① and pour over steaks ②. Turn steaks in marinade and let stand at room temperature for 1 hour.

Drain and place steaks in a greased grill rack ③ 4 inches above gray coals. (Make sure the grill is well greased to keep fish from sticking; a grill basket makes it easier to turn steaks.) Grill 8 to 10 minutes on each side. Serve with lemon or lime wedges, chunks of crusty bread toasted on the grill, a Greek salad with black olives and feta cheese, and roasted red peppers splashed with olive oil.

YIELD
4 servings

PREPARATION
15 minutes

GRILLING
15 minutes

INGREDIENTS
2 pounds ground chuck
2 teaspoons salt
1/4 teaspoon pepper
1/2 teaspoon each marjoram and sage
4 Kaiser rolls
1/4 cup butter or margarine
1 clove garlic, minced
1/2 teaspoon onion salt
1/3 cup catsup
1 tablespoon white prepared
   horseradish

FILLINGS
4 thin slices onion; or 4 small slices
   cheese (cheddar, swiss, or blue); or
8 green or black olives, sliced; or
1/2 cup well-drained sauerkraut

Mix chuck, salt, pepper, marjoram, and sage. Cut meat into 8 pieces and shape each piece into a round burger about 1/2 inch thick ①.

Top 4 of the burgers with the desired filling ②. Cover with remaining burgers and pinch edges together ③.

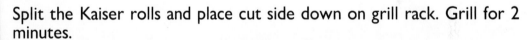

Place burgers 6 inches above gray coals and grill for 5 to 6 minutes on each side.

Split the Kaiser rolls and place cut side down on grill rack. Grill for 2 minutes.

Melt the butter and stir in the garlic and onion salt. Turn the rolls and brush toasted side with garlic butter. Toast rolls another 2 minutes and brush other side with butter.

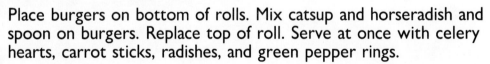

Place burgers on bottom of rolls. Mix catsup and horseradish and spoon on burgers. Replace top of roll. Serve at once with celery hearts, carrot sticks, radishes, and green pepper rings.

23

GREEK GRILLED LEG OF LAMB

YIELD
6 servings

PREPARATION
15 minutes

MARINATING
Overnight

GRILLING
45 minutes

INGREDIENTS
1 leg of lamb, about 5 to 6 pounds
1 cup olive oil
1 cup dry white wine
1 teaspoon each thyme and oregano
2 teaspoons salt
½ teaspoon pepper
½ teaspoon rosemary
2 cloves garlic, minced
2 teaspoons chopped mint leaves

Bone the leg of lamb ①, or have your butcher do it for you. Pound lamb until it is an even thickness ②. Place lamb in a shallow glass dish.

Mix remaining ingredients until well blended and pour over lamb ③. Turn meat in marinade, cover, and marinate in refrigerator overnight.

Drain lamb and reserve marinade. Place meat on grill 6 inches above gray coals and grill for 40 to 45 minutes, brushing with marinade and turning every 10 minutes.

Cut meat into thin slices (lamb will be pink) and sprinkle with chopped fresh mint. Serve with buttered noodles mixed with chopped olives and parsley and foil-baked carrots and oranges.

YIELD
6 servings

PREPARATION
30 minutes

MARINATING
2 hours

GRILLING
30 minutes

INGREDIENTS
3 stalks celery, approximately
4 large onions, approximately
3 cups dry red wine, such as Chianti
1 can (10½ ounces) condensed beef
   broth
1 can (6 ounces) tomato paste
2 tablespoons Worcestershire sauce
2 cups chili sauce
1 boneless chuck steak, about 3
   pounds
12 hero rolls, split

Finely chop the celery so that you have 2 cups; chop the onions finely to have 2 cups ①.

Mix onions and celery with wine, beef broth concentrate, tomato paste, Worcestershire sauce, and chili sauce until well blended. Cook mixture in a saucepan for 20 to 25 minutes, then press mixture through a sieve ②. Cool.

Place chuck steak in a shallow pan or glass dish. Pour marinade over top. Turn steak in marinade several times ③ and allow to marinate for 2 hours at room temperature.

Drain the steak, reserving the marinade. Place steak on grill 6 inches above gray coals. Grill 30 minutes, brushing with marinade and turning every 5 minutes.

Heat the remaining marinade and keep warm. Toast rolls on grill.

Cut the beef into paper-thin slices and place on rolls. Spoon hot marinade over meat and replace tops of buns. Serve at once with potato salad, three-bean salad, and grilled whole frying peppers.

12

YIELD
4 servings

PREPARATION
15 minutes

GRILLING
1 hour, 40 minutes

INGREDIENTS

1 duckling (about 4 pounds), thawed
   if frozen
Salt
1 onion, minced
1 can (8 ounces) tomato sauce
1 tablespoon prepared mustard
1 teaspoon salt
2 tablespoons red wine vinegar
2 tablespoons firmly packed dark
   brown sugar
1 tablespoon Worcestershire sauce

Cut duckling into quarters ① ②. Sprinkle pieces with salt. Trim off all excess skin and fat.

Place pieces of duckling on a large square of heavy-duty foil. Seal packet ③ and place on grill 8 inches above gray coals and cook for 1 hour, turning packet every 10 minutes.

Combine remaining ingredients in a bowl and mix until well blended.

Remove duckling from foil and drain well on paper towels. Brush with sauce and grill another 30 to 40 minutes or until crusty. Brush with sauce and turn every 10 minutes. Serve with cooked rice with raisins and slices of ripe mango or papaya.

YIELD
4 servings

PREPARATION
20 minutes

MARINATING
2 hours

GRILLING
10 minutes

INGREDIENTS
1 flank steak, about 2 pounds
Seasoned instant meat tenderizer
1 clove garlic, mashed
4 scallions, minced
1 cup dry sherry
1 cup Japanese soy sauce
¼ cup tomato paste
8 slices monterey jack cheese
8 cling peach halves

Pound flank steak until it is ½ inch thick ①.

Sprinkle the meat with tenderizer, garlic, and scallions. Roll up meat lengthwise tightly like a jelly roll ②.

Cut meat roll into 8 slices and spear each slice on a skewer ③.

Place skewers into a shallow glass dish. Mix sherry, soy sauce, and tomato paste until smooth; pour over meat. Turn skewers and let marinate for 2 hours at room temperature.

Drain skewers and reserve marinade. Place skewers 4 inches above gray coals and grill for 5 minutes on each side, brushing with marinade every few minutes.

Dip the cheese slices into the marinade and place over meat. Grill until cheese melts.

Dip the peaches into the marinade and grill for 2 to 3 minutes on each side. Serve with hot pita bread and a green bean and red onion salad.

GRILL-BAKED SEA BASS

YIELD
4 servings

PREPARATION
15 minutes

GRILLING
40 minutes

INGREDIENTS
4 pound sea bass, scaled and cleaned
1/3 cup melted butter or margarine
Juice of 1 lemon or lime
1/2 cup coarsely chopped fresh dill
Salt, paprika, garlic powder, onion
    powder

Wash fish and pat dry.

Brush some of the butter on a piece of heavy-duty foil large enough to hold fish ①. Place fish on foil and brush with remaining butter and lemon juice ②. Sprinkle evenly with dill, salt, paprika, garlic powder and onion powder ③.

Seal foil into a packet and place 8 inches above gray coals. Grill for 35 to 40 minutes, turning packet every 10 minutes. Serve with lemon wedges, foil-baked new potatoes and sliced onions, stir-fried mushrooms, and peas.

NOTE *Other fish that can be used for this recipe include black bass, red snapper, striped bass.*

15

YIELD

10 to 12 servings

PREPARATION

30 minutes

GRILLING

5 hours

INGREDIENTS

1 fresh ham, about 10 pounds
1 cup bourbon
1 cup firmly packed brown sugar
½ teaspoon ground cloves
Grated rind of 1 orange
⅓ cup steak sauce

Trim rind from ham and score fat into diamonds ①.

Mix remaining ingredients in a bowl.

Tie ham every 2 inches with string ②. Spear ham on rotisserie rod and fasten ends. If desired, insert a meat thermometer in the center of the thickest part of the ham not touching a bone.

Make a drip pan ③ and place it in grill and arrange coals around it. Place ham 8 inches above gray coals and grill for 4 to 5 hours, adding more coals when needed.

During the last hour of grilling, brush glaze over all sides of ham. Brush with glaze every 10 minutes. Remove from rod and cut into thin slices. Serve with hot sauerkraut, skillet hash browns, and a pickled beet salad with caraway seeds.

NOTE *If using a meat thermometer, allow the ham to cook until it registers 170°F. This ham can also be roasted very successfully in a dome-type covered grill. See manufacturer's instructions for directions.*

ORANGE-GRILLED GAME HENS

YIELD
6 servings

PREPARATION
10 minutes

MARINATING
Overnight

GRILLING
40 minutes

INGREDIENTS
6 Cornish game hens (thawed if
 frozen)
Salt and pepper
¼ cup corn oil
⅔ cup Japanese soy sauce
¼ cup firmly packed dark brown
 sugar
¼ cup frozen orange juice
 concentrate
1 teaspoon ground ginger
2 cloves garlic, mashed

SAUCE
½ cup orange juice concentrate
1 can (8 ounces) tomato sauce
1 tablespoon instant minced onion
1 cup beef broth

Split the game hens ①. Place side by side in a shallow glass pan, and sprinkle with salt and pepper ②.

Mix oil, soy sauce, brown sugar, orange juice, ginger, and garlic; pour over hens ③. Let marinate in refrigerator for 4 hours or overnight.

Drain hens and place on grill 8 inches above gray coals, bone side down, and grill 35 to 40 minutes. Turn hens every 10 minutes, and brush with marinade every time hens are turned.

In a saucepan, combine sauce ingredients and heat on grill until bubbling. Spoon sauce over hens. Serve with hot bacony potato salad, sliced tomatoes, and cucumbers.

YIELD
4 servings

PREPARATION
30 minutes

MARINATING
1 hour

GRILLING
10 minutes

INGREDIENTS
2 pounds raw shrimp
1 cup olive oil
1 teaspoon salt
½ teaspoon Tabasco
2 cloves garlic, mashed
Juice of 1 lemon
1 teaspoon oregano
¼ cup chili sauce

Shell and devein shrimp but leave tail shell attached ① ②.

In a bowl, mix shrimp with remaining ingredients until well blended ③, and let marinate for 1 hour at room temperature.

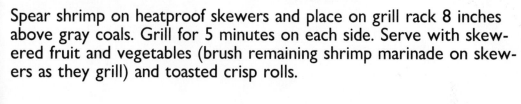

Spear shrimp on heatproof skewers and place on grill rack 8 inches above gray coals. Grill for 5 minutes on each side. Serve with skewered fruit and vegetables (brush remaining shrimp marinade on skewers as they grill) and toasted crisp rolls.

YIELD
6 servings

PREPARATION
20 minutes

SOAKING/ MARINATING
1 hour

GRILLING
20 minutes

INGREDIENTS
6 round-bone shoulder lamb chops,
   cut 1 inch thick
12 brown-and-serve sausages
6 lamb kidneys
12 slices bacon
12 large mushrooms
6 tomatoes
Salt and pepper

MUSTARD MARINADE
1 tablespoon dry mustard
1 cup beef broth
1 cup Japanese soy sauce
½ cup firmly packed brown sugar
1 cup ale

Slash the fatty edges of the chops to prevent curling.

Thaw sausages, if they are frozen.

Cut the kidneys in half horizontally ①, then soak for 1 hour in cold water with 1 tablespoon of vinegar added. Drain and pat dry.

Wrap the kidney halves in bacon ② and fasten with a toothpick.

Mix marinade ingredients in a large bowl, stirring until sugar is dissolved. Add meats and let marinate 1 hour.

Trim the mushrooms and cut the tomatoes in half ③. Sprinkle with salt and pepper.

Drain meats and place on grill 8 inches above gray coals. Grill the chops for 20 minutes; grill the kidneys for 20 minutes or until bacon is crisp; grill sausages for 15 minutes; and grill vegetables for 10 minutes. Brush vegetables while they are on the grill with some of the marinade. If desired, marinade may be brushed on meats every 5 minutes during grilling.

Serve meats on toast triangles, with foil-baked potatoes and green cabbage.

19

YIELD
8 servings

PREPARATION
10 minutes

GRILLING
1 hour

INGREDIENTS
8 pounds pork spareribs
Salt and pepper
½ green bell pepper
⅓ cup corn oil
2 teaspoons salt
3 cloves garlic, minced
2 cans (6 ounces each) frozen
    pineapple juice concentrate
1 cup firmly packed light brown sugar
1½ cups red wine vinegar
¼ cup soy sauce

Trim excess fat from the underside of the ribs ①. Cut into 2 rib sections ②, then sprinkle pieces with salt and pepper.

Mince the green pepper so you have ⅓ cup ③. Combine with remaining ingredients in a saucepan and place on grill. Simmer for 5 minutes.

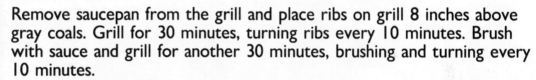

Remove saucepan from the grill and place ribs on grill 8 inches above gray coals. Grill for 30 minutes, turning ribs every 10 minutes. Brush with sauce and grill for another 30 minutes, brushing and turning every 10 minutes.

Heat any remaining sauce and serve spooned over the ribs. Have plenty of napkins handy, as this is a sloppy, delicious dish. Serve with macaroni salad, grilled mushrooms, and foil-baked peas.

YIELD

4 servings

PREPARATION

15 minutes

GRILLING

10 minutes

INGREDIENTS

1 pound cocktail frankfurters
1 can (1 pound) boiled onions, drained
2 green peppers, cut into 1-inch squares
4 pineapple slices, quartered
8 cherry tomatoes
1 cup pineapple juice
¼ cup firmly packed brown sugar
¼ cup prepared mustard

Alternately spear the frankfurters, onions, peppers, pineapple quarters, and tomatoes on heatproof skewers ①.

Mix the pineapple juice, brown sugar, and mustard ②. Brush mixture on the skewers ③.

Place kabobs on the grill 8 inches above gray coals and grill for 10 to 12 minutes, turning and brushing with sauce every 2 to 3 minutes. Serve with hot bacon-potato salad or a tossed salad of bean sprouts, pea pods, scallions, and celery slices.

21

YIELD
4 servings

PREPARATION
45 minutes

STEAMING
40 minutes

INGREDIENTS
1 chicken, about 3 pounds, quartered
Salt and pepper
2 large onions
4 ears corn
6 dozen steamer clams or littleneck
    clams

HOT SAUCE
1 cup catsup
¼ cup horseradish
1 tablespoon lemon juice

You will need a steamer pot. The bottom holds the water about 2 inches deep and the top has a perforated bottom to allow steam to enter and cook the food. The steamer can be placed directly on the coals or on the lowest setting of the grill rack, but to make the water boil quicker, bring it to a boil in the kitchen and then place steamer on the grill.

Sprinkle chicken with salt and pepper. Cut onion into quarters ①. Place chicken into steamer along with the onions. Cover and steam for 20 minutes.

Scrub the clams and shuck the corn ②. Add to the steamer, cover, and steam for another 20 minutes, or until the clams are open.

Mix the catsup, horseradish, and lemon juice and place into a bowl for dipping clams ③. Serve with melted butter, lemon wedges, crusty bread, and cold beer.

YIELD
6 servings

PREPARATION
20 minutes

MARINATING
1 hour

GRILLING
30 minutes

INGREDIENTS
3 pounds boneless pork or beef
3 navel oranges
2 red bell peppers
1 cup bottled barbecue sauce
1 cup tomato purée
½ cup minced celery
1 small onion, minced
¼ cup smooth peanut butter
⅓ cup water
1 tablespoon sesame seeds, toasted

Cut the meat into ¼-inch-thick strips ①. Cut the oranges into wedges ②. Seed and cut the peppers into 1-inch strips. Thread the beef, orange wedges, and peppers on heatproof skewers ③.

Mix the remaining ingredients except the sesame seeds, until well blended. Place skewers into a shallow dish. Pour sauce over them. Turn skewers in the sauce, then let marinate for 1 hour at room temperature.

Drain skewers and place on grill 6 inches above gray coals. Grill for 30 minutes, turning and brushing with sauce every 5 minutes.

If any sauce remains, heat it on the grill and spoon it over each serving. Sprinkle with toasted sesame seeds, and serve with toasted squares of firm tofu splashed with hoisin sauce, pickled cherry peppers, and crisp romaine topped with straw mushrooms.

YIELD
8 servings

PREPARATION
10 minutes

GRILLING
3 hours

INGREDIENTS
1 turkey, about 10 pounds, thawed if
   frozen
Salt and pepper
½ cup melted butter or margarine
2 cloves garlic, mashed
Juice of 1 lemon and 1 orange
1 cup jellied cranberry sauce, mashed
¼ cup prepared mustard
¼ cup honey

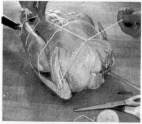

Build the fire arranging the coals at the back of the rotisserie and with a long, narrow drip pan at the front.

Sprinkle turkey inside and out with salt and pepper. Pass the rotisserie rod through the neck skin and then to a point just above the tail ①. Fasten ends. Tie wings and legs close to the body with string ②. If desired, place a meat thermometer into the thickest part of the thigh, not touching a bone ③.

Place turkey 8 inches above gray coals and let rotate for 2 to 2½ hours, adding more coals from time to time.

Combine remaining ingredients and brush over turkey every 5 minutes. Grill for another 30 to 40 minutes or until richly browned.

If any sauce remains, heat it in a pan on the grill and spoon over each serving. Serve with brown-and-serve biscuits baked on grill, foil-baked succotash, and baked sweet potatoes.

This turkey can also be made very successfully on a dome-type covered grill. See manufacturer's instructions for specifics.

NOTE *If you are using a meat thermometer, allow turkey to cook until it registers 180°F.*

YIELD
4 servings

PREPARATION
15 minutes

MARINATING
2 hours

GRILLING
20 minutes

INGREDIENTS
1 small pineapple
2 pounds boneless lamb (cut from leg)
2 Granny Smith apples
1 cup Italian salad dressing
2 teaspoons curry powder
Juice of 1 lime
¼ teaspoon pepper

Cut away outside edge from the pineapple ①, then core and cut into 1½-inch chunks. Cut the meat into 1-inch chunks. Halve and core the apples and cut into thick wedges.

In a large bowl, mix fruit, lamb, and remaining ingredients ②. Let marinate for 2 hours at room temperature.

Drain meat and fruit and thread alternating cubes of meat, pineapple, and apple on heatproof skewers ③. Place kabobs 8 inches above gray coals and grill for 15 to 20 minutes, brushing with marinade every 5 minutes. Turn skewers each time they are brushed.

If any marinade remains, spoon it over the kabobs, and serve on a bed of saffron rice sprinkled with toasted slivered almonds and with a crisp, tossed green salad.

YIELD
6 servings

PREPARATION
5 minutes

GRILLING
12 minutes

INGREDIENTS
3 (smoked) ham steaks, each 1 inch
  thick
Ground cloves
1/2 cup firmly packed light brown
  sugar

Cut ham steaks in half ① and sprinkle each piece lightly with ground cloves ②.

Place steaks on grill 8 inches above gray coals, and broil 5 minutes on each side.

Spread one side with about 1 tablespoon of brown sugar ③ and turn. Grill for 1 minute, then spread other side with sugar and turn again. Grill for 1 minute. Serve with baked sweet potatoes and grilled pineapple quarters brushed with honey.

YIELD
6 servings

PREPARATION
10 minutes

GRILLING
40 minutes

INGREDIENTS
3 pound-piece large bologna
Whole cloves
¼ cup corn oil
⅓ cup cider vinegar
1 cup catsup
¼ cup steak sauce
¼ cup sugar
1 small onion, minced
½ teaspoon hot pepper sauce

26

Remove casing from bologna ① and leave whole. Spear the bologna on a rotisserie rod and fasten the ends. Make diagonal cuts ¼ inch deep into the bologna on all sides ②. Press the cloves 2 inches apart into the cuts ③.

Mix the remaining ingredients and place in saucepan on top of grill. Place rotisserie in place and rotate 8 inches above gray coals. Brush bologna with sauce every 10 minutes. Grill for 30 to 40 minutes.

Remove bologna from the spear and cut into thin slices. If any sauce remains, heat it and spoon it over each serving. Serve with chunks of sesame-seed Italian bread, red onion slices, and roasted baby eggplants.

NOTE *This roast can also be cooked with a Sweet Hot Glaze. To prepare this glaze, place 1 cup of red currant jelly and ¼ cup prepared mustard in a saucepan on the grill and stir until jelly is melted and mixture is smooth. Brush on bologna every 10 minutes.*

YIELD
6 servings each

PREPARATION
10–20 minutes

GRILLING
10–50 minutes

FOIL-BAKED CORN

Shuck 6 ears of corn and place each ear on a square of heavy-duty foil. Top corn with 6 tablespoons butter, 1½ teaspoons sugar, a sprinkling of curry powder, and some red pepper flakes. Shape foil into packets, seal, and place on grill 6 inches above gray coals. Grill for 10 to 15 minutes, turning packets every 5 minutes.

GRILLED SQUASH PARMESAN

Place 3 sliced zucchini, 2 diced tomatoes, ½ teaspoon oregano, ½ teaspoon salt, and 3 tablespoons grated Parmesan cheese on a large square of heavy-duty foil (1). Top with 3 tablespoons butter. Shape foil into packet, seal, and place 6 inches above gray coals. Grill 20 to 25 minutes, turning packet every 10 minutes.

CAULIFLOWER POLONAISE

Place 1 cauliflower (broken into flowerets), ½ cup salted peanuts, and ½ cup shredded sharp cheddar cheese on a large square of heavy-duty foil. Add ½ cup well-seasoned chicken broth. Seal foil into packet and place on grill 6 inches above gray coals. Grill for 20 to 25 minutes, turning packet every 10 minutes.

STUFFED MUSHROOMS

Stuff 24 mushroom caps with a mixture of 2 tablespoons butter, 2 teaspoons instant minced onion, 1 cup grated sharp cheddar cheese, ¼ cup bacon bits, ½ cup fresh bread crumbs, and 2 tablespoons chopped parsley. Place 4 mushrooms on each square of heavy-duty foil and seal foil into packets (2). Place on grill 6 inches above gray coals and grill for 12 to 15 minutes. Do not turn packets.

FRENCH-STYLE PEAS

Place 2 unwrapped packages of frozen peas on a large square of heavy-duty foil. Top with ¼ cup butter, 4 shredded lettuce leaves, ½ teaspoon sugar, and a light sprinkling of salt and pepper (3). Seal foil into packets and place on grill 8 inches above gray coals. Grill for 10 to 15 minutes, turning packet every 5 minutes.

MICKIES

Place scrubbed Idaho potatoes on grill 6 inches above gray coals and grill for 40 to 50 minutes, or until potatoes are easily pierced and skins are crusty and black. Turn potatoes every 5 minutes. Serve split open and topped with a mixture of 1 cup sour cream and 3 tablespoons chopped chives. (Sweet potatoes or yams may be baked in the same way, only topped with ½ cup apricot preserves mixed with ¼ cup melted butter.)

YIELD
6 servings each

PREPARATION
10–20 minutes

GRILLING
5–40 minutes

BAKED AMARETTO APPLES

Peel and core 6 Granny Smith or Rome Beauty apples, leaving them whole ①. Place each on a square of heavy-duty foil and fill center with 6 tablespoons orange marmalade. Sprinkle with 6 tablespoons slivered almonds and 6 tablespoons Amaretto liqueur. Dot with 6 tablespoons butter and seal foil into packets. Place 8 inches above gray coals and grill for 35 to 40 minutes, turning every 10 minutes. Length of cooking depends on size of apple; apples should be easily pierced.

RUM BANANAS

Place 6 peeled firm bananas on a large square of heavy-duty foil and top with a mixture of ⅓ cup firmly packed dark brown sugar, ¼ cup dark rum, and ½ teaspoon cinnamon ②. Dot top with 3 tablespoons butter and seal foil into a packet. Place 8 inches above gray coals and grill for 10 to 15 minutes, turning packet every 5 minutes. Serve hot topped with whipped cream.

HOT FRUIT SAUCE FOR ICE CREAM

Place 1 cup each diced pineapple, seedless green grapes, sliced peaches, mandarin oranges, diced apple, and chopped pitted dates on a large square of heavy-duty foil. Add ½ cup pineapple preserves, ½ teaspoon ground ginger, and ¼ cup cream sherry ③. Seal foil into a packet and place 8 inches above gray coals. Grill for 15 to 20 minutes, turning packet every 10 minutes. Serve hot, spooned over ice cream.

BRANDIED PEARS WITH HOT FUDGE SAUCE

Place 6 pears—peeled, halved, and cored—on a large square of heavy-duty foil. Add juice of 1 lemon, ½ cup sugar, and ¼ cup brandy. Seal foil into packets and place 8 inches above gray coals. Grill for 15 to 20 minutes, turning packet every 5 minutes.

In a saucepan on grill, combine 1 cup chocolate syrup, 1 tablespoon instant coffee, and ⅓ cup orange liqueur. Heat until bubbly, then serve pears with hot sauce.

GRILLED PEACHES

Peel and halve 6 firm peaches. Remove pit and brush with melted butter. Place cut side down 6 inches above gray coals and grill for 2 to 3 minutes on each side or until lightly brown. In a small skillet, melt 2 tablespoons butter and stir in 6 tablespoons firmly packed brown sugar. Serve peaches topped with sugar mixture and then top with sour cream or vanilla yogurt.

GRILLED PINEAPPLE

Peel 1 large pineapple and cut into 6 thick crosswise slices. Brush slices with honey and let stand for 30 minutes. Brush with melted butter on all sides and grill 6 inches above gray coals for 4 to 5 minutes on each side.

MUSTARD-BARBECUED RIBS RECIPE

29

YIELD
6 servings

PREPARATION
10 minutes

GRILLING
1 hour

INGREDIENTS
6 pounds spareribs
1 cup butter or margarine
3 tablespoons dry mustard
3 tablespoons cider vinegar
2 cups chicken broth

Trim fat from ribs. Leave ribs in 1 piece or cut into 2 rib sections.

Place ribs on grill 8 inches above gray coals and grill for 30 minutes, turning ribs every 10 minutes.

Combine remaining ingredients in a saucepan and place on grill rack. Stir mixture until butter is melted and sauce is smooth.

Brush the sauce on the ribs and grill for another 30 minutes. Brush with sauce every 5 minutes and turn. Serve with baked beans, warmed cornbread, and grilled whole plum tomatoes.

SPICY CHICKEN RECIPE

30

YIELD
6 servings

PREPARATION
15 minutes

GRILLING
40 minutes

INGREDIENTS
3 broiler-fryers, about 2 lbs each, quartered
Salt and pepper
1/2 cup butter or margarine
1 clove garlic, minced
1 onion, minced
1 cup chili sauce
1 tablespoon prepared mustard
1 tablespoon prepared horseradish
1 tablespoon Worcestershire sauce
1 teaspoon salt
Juice of 1 lemon
1 tablespoon sugar
1/2 teaspoon each marjoram and thyme
1/4 teaspoon pepper
2 cups water

Sprinkle chicken with salt and pepper. Set aside.

Place remaining ingredients in a saucepan 4 inches above gray coals and stir until sauce bubbles. Simmer for 20 minutes. Remove from grill.

Place chicken on grill 8 inches above gray coals and grill for 35 to 40 minutes, turning and basting with sauce every 10 minutes.

Heat any sauce remaining and spoon over each serving. Serve with baked potatoes topped with cheddar cheese and a fresh fruit salad.

SPICY INDIAN PORK SKEWERS

YIELD

6 servings

PREPARATION

20 minutes

MARINATING

Overnight

GRILLING

35 minutes

INGREDIENTS

3 pounds boneless pork, cut into 1-inch cubes
1 cup olive oil
¼ cup lemon juice
¼ cup red wine vinegar
1 tablespoon curry powder
2 cloves garlic, mashed

1½ teaspoons salt
1 eggplant, peeled and cut into 1½-inch cubes
2 tart apples, cored and cut into thick wedges
12 small whole onions, parboiled for 5 minutes

In a bowl, mix pork, olive oil, lemon juice, vinegar, curry powder, garlic, and salt. Cover and refrigerate overnight.

Add eggplant, apples, and onions to marinade mixture and stir to coat.

Alternately spear the pork, eggplant, apples, and onions on heatproof skewers. Reserve the marinade.

Place the skewers on the grill 8 inches above gray coals and grill 30 to 35 minutes, turning and brushing with marinade every 5 minutes. Serve with curried rice with raisins and almonds and grilled bananas.

TERIYAKI BEEF OR CHICKEN

YIELD

6 servings

PREPARATION

20 minutes

MARINATING

2 hours

INGREDIENTS

3 pounds beef sirloin or boneless and skinless chicken breasts, cut into 1½-inch cubes
1 cup dry sherry
1 cup Japanese soy sauce

1 teaspoon ground ginger
1 teaspoon garlic powder
¼ teaspoon pepper
1 large pineapple, peeled and cut into 6 thick slices

Place beef or chicken cubes into a large bowl and add sherry, soy sauce, ginger, garlic powder, and pepper. Let marinate at room temperature for 2 hours. Drain meat, reserving marinade.

Spear the beef or chicken cubes on heatproof skewers. Place skewers 6 inches above gray coals and grill for 10 minutes, turning and brushing skewers with reserved marinade.

Brush pineapple slices with marinade and grill for 3 minutes on each side. Heat any remaining marinade and serve as a dip.

INDEX

Apples, Baked Amaretto, 60–61

Bananas, Rum, 60–61
Beef:
    Indonesian Satés, 48–49
    London Broil Pinwheels, 30–31
    Minute Steak Roll-ups, 14–15
    Salt-and pepper-crusted Steak, 6–7
    Surprise Burgers on Garlic Rolls, 22–23
    Teriyaki Beef, 63
    Texas Barbecued Beef, 26–27

Cauliflower Polonaise, 58–59
Chicken:
    Clambake on the Grill, 46–47
    Diablo Chicken Wings, 10–11
    Spicy Chicken, 62
    Teriyaki Chicken, 63
    with 3 Bastes, 16–17
Clambake on the Grill, 46–47
Corn, Foil-baked, 58–59

Duck, Savory Barbecued, 28–29

Fish:
    Grill-baked Sea Bass, 32–33
    Mediterranean Swordfish Steaks, 20–21
Franks:
    Quick and Easy Kabobs, 44–45
    Saucy Stuffed, 12–13
Fruit:
    Grilled, 60–61
    Sauce, Hot, for Ice Cream, 60–61

Game Hens, Orange-grilled, 36–37

Ham:
    Bourbon-glazed Fresh, 34–35
    Sugar-grilled Steak, 54–55

Kidneys: English Mixed Grill, 40–41
Lamb:
    Curry-glazed Lamb and Apple Kabobs, 52–53
    English Mixed Grill, 40–41
    Greek Grilled Leg of, 24–25

Mickies (potatoes), 58–59
Mushrooms, Stuffed, 58–59

Peaches, Grilled, 60–61
Pears, Brandied, with Hot Fudge Sauce, 60–61
Peas, French-style, 58–59
Pineapple, Grilled, 60–61
Pork:
    Bourbon-glazed Fresh Ham, 34–35
    Indonesian Satés, 48–49
    Mexican Country Back Ribs, 8–9
    Mustard-barbecued Ribs, 62
    Spicy Indian Pork Skewers, 63
    Spit-roasted Bologna, 56–57
    Sugar-grilled Ham Steak, 54–55
    Sweet and Sour Spareribs, 42–43
    SEE ALSO Franks, Sausages
Potatoes (Mickies), 56–57

Sausages:
    English Mixed Grill, 40–41
    Polish Sausage and Pepper Heros, 18–19
Sea Bass, Grilled-baked, 32–33
Shrimp, Barbecued Spicy, 38–39
Squash, Parmesan Grilled, 58–59
Swordfish Steak, Mediterranean, 20–21

Turkey, Barbecued Rotisserie, 50–51

Vegetables, Grilled, 58–59